Christmas Kitties for You. Copyright © 2024 by Kitty Books

ISBN: 9789189848948

All Rights Reserved. No part of this work may be reproduced, incorporated into a computer system, or transmitted in any form or by any means (electronic, mechanical, photocopying, recording or otherwise) without the prior written permission of the copyright holders. Infringement of such rights may constitute an intellectual property crime.

In winter's cold and festive sights, A kitten's warmth lights up the nights.

With every purr and playful glance, Christmas magic has its chance.

Whiskers twitch and stockings tear, Santa Claws has been right there.

Paws on the presents, tail in the way, cats make Christmas every day.

In the joy of Christmas Eve, A cats love helps us believe.

Santa Claws brings joy and cheer, With purrs and whiskers, love is near.

In holiday lights and festive glow, A kitty's charm continues to grow.

Christmas night with purring delight, cats make everything feel just right.

Amid the tinsel and the tree, A cat's delight is plain to see.

With purrs that warm the coldest night, A cat makes everything feel right.

With gentle paws and cozy naps, Christmas joy fills every lapse.

No snow required, just whiskers and cheer, cats make the best of the year.

Wrapped in joy and holiday cheer, Kitty love is always near.

A Christmas turkey can't survive, when curious cats take a dive.

A whiskered wish for all to hear: A meowy Christmas and a purr-filled year!

Amid the laughter and the light, A kitty's love makes everything right.

Under the lights with whiskers aglow, cats spread joy more than you know.

With purrs as soft as falling snow, A kitten's affection continues to show.

Snowflakes fall, and hearts take flight, A cat's love is warm and bright.

From tree to gift, their mission's clear: cats make Christmas the best of the year.

A Christmas star with paws and fluff, cats prove love is gift enough.

No need for elves when cats are near, they bring the joy and holiday cheer.

Tiny paws on a shopping spree, filling the list with gifts for thee.

Beneath the mistletoe so green, A cat's affection can be seen.

Holiday magic in the air, A cats purr brings love to share.

Under the lights with eyes aglow, cats make Christmas magic flow.

With jingling bells and a meowy cheer, kittens sing carols for all to hear.

Tails swish near cookies so sweet, Christmas cats make gingerbread their treat.

Milton Keynes UK
Ingram Content Group UK Ltd.
UKHW050431041224
452080UK00019B/171